How Much Unemployment?

The methods and measures dissected

JOHN B. WOOD

Published by
THE INSTITUTE OF ECONOMIC AFFAIRS
1972

First published April 1972
© THE INSTITUTE OF ECONOMIC AFFAIRS

SBN 255   36032-0

Printed in Great Britain by
Eastbourne Printers Limited, Eastbourne, Sussex
Set in Univers 9 on 10 pt. Series 689

Contents

CHARTS   *page*

TABLES

Preface

The Institute was founded in 1957 as a research and educational trust to show the light that economics can throw on business practice and public policy. It is the only independent organisation in Britain that specialises in the micro-economic analysis of existing or potential markets in the private and public sectors of the economy.

IEA studies invariably include the findings of new researches. In the *Hobart Papers* and some other series the focus of interest is on the author's analysis and recommendations for policy. In others empirical research is the primary contribution. Earlier *Research Monographs* have examined the consequences of professional and trade union restrictions, state monopoly in roads and nuclear energy, transport licensing and agricultural marketing, central direction in welfare and poverty policy and of economic planning and governmental forecasting.

Some years ago the Institute considered the uncritical acceptance, even in academic circles and journalism, of indicators commonly used to reveal the supposed state of the economy. It was discussed with the late John R. Applebey, a brilliant economic journalist on *The Financial Times* and *The Daily Telegraph* who sadly and suddenly died at an early age. A series of studies was intended to reveal the economic significance—or insignificance—of total production (which Mr Applebey was to analyse), 'the' price level, national income, national expenditure, total imports and exports, and other macro-economic aggregates or averages.

Difficulty in finding suitable authors has delayed publication of the first study until Research Monograph 28 by Mr John B. Wood. His chosen subject is the national statistics—or rather statistic—on unemployment, although his analysis indicates by implication the weaknesses of other macro-economic measures, the errors they can create in government and the public mind, and the urgency of interpreting them in micro-economic terms by breaking them down into their component quantities and activities which have economic significance.

6

Mr Wood's analysis reflects the characteristic approach of the Institute since its foundation. Macro-economics has a useful role to play in economic analysis and application, but, perhaps because it has been of recent growth, it has been adopted uncritically without adequate discussions of its defects in theory and practice. Institute Papers by Dr Malcolm Fisher[1] in 1964 and Professor E. W. Streissler[2] in 1970 were efforts to inform economists, students and others of the limitations as well as the uses of macro-economic theory, models, and forecasting. Mr Wood's *Monograph* confirms, by its careful dissection of the statistic of unemployment and its analysis by duration, region, industry, and sex, that it has become a questionable, if not harmful, instrument in guiding economic policy. (His Chart 1 dramatically, in a *coup d'oeil*, shows the thin layer of the total of 'unemployment' that is long-term unemployable in black shading into the top layer of 're-deploy-able' in white.) Since 1944, when the objective of 'a high and stable level of employment' was laid down by economists in government service and accepted by the coalition government, and the writings of Lord Beveridge on 'full employment', the statistic of unemploy-ment has become a totem pole of British economic policy—and often not much more scientific. In the 1944 *Full Employment in a Free Society* Beveridge put 'full employment at 3 per cent' as 'a conservative, rather than a hopeful aim'. Keynes said 'No harm in aiming at 3 per cent unemployed, but I shall be surprised if we succeed'. Hugh Gaitskell in 1951 defined 'full employment' as 3 per cent unemployment 'at the seasonal peak'. In contrast Professor John Jewkes thought 'Unemployment of 5 or 6 per cent should not be a matter of concern'. The less precise the per-centage definitions, the more scholarly they are; the more precise, the more precarious.

Mr Wood shows that even the total of 'unemployed' is calculated in a misleading fashion as a percentage of a population that excludes a large part of economically active people. He emphasises that unemployment and employment are not technical quantities but economic variables that respond to the price of labour in the market (in so far as government provides it with the required framework of law and it is not obstructed by trade union monopoly). He argues that unemployment, even if accurately defined and closely examined for its significant elements, may be less impor-tant, in studying the state of the economy, than employment. He traces the changes in the labour market since 1966 and argues that

[1]*Macro-Economic Models: Nature, Purpose and Limitations,* Eaton Paper 2, IEA, 1964 (out of print).
[2]*Pitfalls in Econometric Forecasting,* Research Monograph 23, IEA, 1970.

even more important than the more recent rise in 'unemployment' is the reduction of the labour force of approaching $1\frac{1}{2}$ million. He discusses types of unemployment and employment frequently over-looked by economists and policy-makers—hidden employment as well as 'hidden unemployment', emphasised recently by sociologists in *New Society* and elsewhere, negative unemployment (which may be the counterpart to over-full employment), voluntary and false unemployment, and other forms.

Perhaps most fundamentally Mr Wood raises questions about the meaning of employment and unemployment that economists have too long ignored in their preoccupation with its measurement, inaccurate and misleading even though that has been. Here Mr Wood returns to an older and neglected tradition of classical analysis revived in the writings of Professor F. A. Hayek and, less well-known, Professor W. H. Hutt, not least the seminal *Theory of Idle Resources.*[1] This part of Mr Wood's analysis will provide economists with much food for thought.

By chance the argument that employment has been relatively neglected in the preoccupation—or obsession—with 'unemployment', and that it is at least as important and may be the more important indicator of the state of the economy, has recently been urged by Mr Geoffrey Moore, US Federal Commissioner for Labor Statistics.[2] He says it would be wrong for three reasons to suppose that unemployment in the USA (6 per cent) and employment (by inference 94 per cent) are obverse sides of the same coin. The conception of employment is less ambiguous than that of unemployment. Unemployment is subject to a larger sampling error than employment; seasonal variations are easier to eliminate in employment. And unemployment reacts more slowly to the 'business cycle' than employment: it is therefore not necessarily evidence of economic improvement or deterioration and it should be checked by observing movements in employment.

The harm that can be done by using the total of unemployment as a guide to the state of the economy prompts the even more fundamental question, put by Professor Milton Friedman,[3] whether unemployment should be 'a numerical goal' of economic policy. There is no more reason why unemployment should be 3 per cent than 2, 4, 5 or 8 per cent so long as the unemployed are not suffering but are being retrained for more productive work. Since the total will vary not only with the state of the economy but also with the capacity of government, industry and individuals to

---

[1] Jonathan Cape, 1939.
[2] *Wall Street Journal,* 3 February, 1972.
[3] *Newsweek,* 31 January, 1972.

arrange retraining, it might be more rational to make unemployment, whether half a million, a million or two millions, a residual from other policies designed to keep the economy employing the 'optimal' amount and kind of resources. Since 'unemployment' does not mean failure to find work but, for many people, the gap between one job and another—which actors euphemise as 'resting'—or between school and work, or housework and (paid) work, government might do better to abandon its fixation on unemployment to concentrate on removing the obstacles—trade union and professional restrictions, subsidised council housing, apprenticeship rules, etc.—to the free movement of labour, assisting the redeployment of workers made redundant by technical and social change, and for the rest refining the monetary and fiscal environment within which the economy can adapt itself rapidly to internal and external conditions. One more false teaching of Beveridge might thus be abandoned, with benefit, not least, to the unemployed.

Mr Wood's study is much more than a statistical dissection of 'unemployment'; it can be read as raising fundamental issues in the nature and significance of employment. The conclusions modestly confine themselves to improvements in the presentation of published statistics and to methods of calculation; but they offer thought-provoking suggestions for fundamental reconsideration of the attitude to the use of unemployment statistics in public discussion and government policy.

The Institute has to thank Professor S. R. Dennison, a Trustee of the Institute and Vice-Chancellor-designate of the University of Hull, and Professor A. A. Walters of the London School of Economics and a member of the Institute's Advisory Council, who read early drafts and whose comments have been taken into account in the final revisions.

Its constitution requires the Institute to dissociate its trustees, directors and advisers from its authors' analyses and conclusions, but it offers Mr Wood's cogent and clearly argued *Monograph* as the first of a series to economists who may be ripe for a reconsideration of the theory of employment and the use of macro- and microeconomic methods, to teachers and students of economics still using text-books largely based on the fashionable economics of the Keynesian epoch, to politicians and civil servants who conservatively persist with economic indicators that do not mean what they say, and to the hard-pressed corps of journalists and broadcasters who must master economic concepts and interpret them without time for reflection or close examination.

March 1972   EDITOR

The Author

JOHN WOOD was born in 1924 and educated at Oundle. He studied Philosophy, Politics and Economics at Oxford and Economics at Cambridge. He has since worked as an economist in the Civil Service—in the Economic Section of the Cabinet secretariat (1944–46); in politics—for the Conservative Research Department (1948–51); in journalism—the City office of the *Manchester Guardian* (1951–53); in the City—with Lazard Brothers (1954–59); and in industry—as head of the economic section of Associated Electrical Industries (1959–67).

He was then for some time a director of a number of industrial companies and a Trustee of the Institute of Economic Affairs, of which he is now Deputy Director.

He has written and broadcast widely on economic affairs, edited a number of books, including a series of political biographies, and is author of two books on shareholding and taxation, and a number of pamphlets, the first of which was for the Conservative Political Centre, in 1951, on *Employment.*

ONE

The Conventional Measures

Introduction

This is not an essay about how unemployment is caused or how it should be cured, but about how it is or should be measured. The former inquiry would have to call in question much of what has been written in economics during the last 40 years. The latter more modest survey may still throw some light on the aetiology of unemployment, or else what's measurement for?

A great deal of statistical material is available from the Department of Employment (the former Ministry of Labour), most of which is broadly comparable since 1948. In the interests of readability many of the Department's qualifications and reservations about their figures (due to administrative changes, or minor alterations in scope and method) are omitted.

The main object is to 'dis-aggregate' the figures in general use. As a description of the complex situation at the end of 1971, 'one million unemployed' makes, to use a North country phrase, 'a better door than a window'. One has to look through to the detail of unemployment by duration, sex, region, age and occupation to reach even a moderate understanding of what is happening. Throughout, the study is limited to Great Britain. The approach is historical rather than analytical.

The British government first committed itself to maintain 'a high and stable level of employment' as long ago as May 1944.[1] But in the 27 years since that commitment there seems to have been no real examination of the criteria by which the success or failure of policy could be judged. It is unfortunate that such a long overdue examination should only be taking place now that memories and emotions are being stirred by the return of substantial unemployment.

This study is in no sense a defence of the present level of unemployment. But how much unemployment is either acceptable, or

---

[1] White Paper on *Employment Policy*, Cmd. 6527, HMSO, 1944. The phrase 'full employment' was not used.

inevitable, depends on what is described as 'unemployment'. Unemployment today is quite different from what it was not only before the last war, but even as recently as five years ago. Inflation has arguably now become by far the greater social evil.

Accuracy of unemployment statistic questioned

As, towards the end of 1971, the number of people reported to be out of work in Great Britain approached one million, conflicting views were put forward about the accuracy of the measures of unemployment. Businessmen who still found it difficult to maintain their labour establishment, citizens frustrated by the inadequacies of public services still blamed on a shortage of staff, naturally felt that the published figures in some way exaggerated the amount of unemployment.[1]

Others, aware of some of the limitations of the figures and pointing to the steady fall in the working population, argued that far more people—perhaps twice as many—were looking for jobs than the statistics recorded.[2]

Economists have so far paid less attention than they might to the conspicuous paradox that even though unemployment was going up, wages and earnings were not going down.

The register

No precise definition exists, or has been sought, of an 'unemployed' person and therefore of 'unemployment'. Anyone who has left school, is not in paid employment, who is available for work and capable of working may register for a job at the local employment exchange. A count every month of those so registered is the measure of the country's 'unemployed'. This system reflects the traditional idea of measuring 'involuntary' unemployment, that is, people who are able and willing to work and 'genuinely' seeking it, but without success. It therefore measures the 'need' for work and not the potential supply of labour in terms of a schedule of 'wages'.

---

[1] 'The big construction firms are all looking for skilled labour, and cannot get anything like enough', reported Paddy McGarvey in the *Sunday Telegraph*, 20 January, 1972. Cf. Peter Jay, 'Where have all the workers gone?', *The Times*, 9 October, 1971.

[2] Cf. Brian Hunter, 'Who are the unemployed?', *New Society*, 23 July, 1970; Guy Standing, 'A million unemployed already?', *New Society*, 14 October, 1971.

The unemployment register may be inadequate—no one is compelled to register; nevertheless it is the only direct source of information and the inevitable starting point for any inquiry.[1] Information from the register becomes available through the Department of Employment's monthly *Gazette*, eventually in a whole series of analyses of unemployment by region, occupation, sex, age and duration. Little of this enters the public discussion, which usually focuses on only one figure—the total register of unemployed, and the percentage it forms of all employees. In December 1971, the total register was 923,000 and the percentage rate was 4.0. These are the 'facts' about unemployment which are used by the press, radio and television, and which therefore condition public opinion, and in turn, policy. These familiar measures are, however, completely unsatisfactory. They are misleading both as indicators of the absolute level of unemployment and the proportion of the labour force out of work.

The total register, for instance, includes a number only temporarily out of work who know they have a job waiting for them. The number can vary between 10,000 and 50,000 but sometimes can be more. During the miners' strike in February 1972, for instance, the number temporarily out of work soared to about 650,000, an exceptional but not unique example (over 200,000 were temporarily stopped during the severe winter of 1962–3).

The register also includes boys and girls who have left school but have not yet found employment. Every year about half a million young people start work for the first time, and the figures, particularly for July, August and September, are always swollen by school-leavers. For many years, between 35,000 and 55,000 school-leavers have been included as 'unemployed' in August and still over 20,000 in September, but by the end of the year the figure is generally down to 3,000 or 4,000.

When these two adjustments are made to the total register, the number of unemployed, taking December 1971, is reduced from 923,000 to 859,000 and the percentage rate from 4.0 to 3.8. This smaller figure is described as the 'wholly unemployed' (though it still includes a small number of casual workers) and is clearly a slightly better measure.

Misleading calculations

The way the 'percentage' rate is calculated is also unsatisfactory, even though it has been in use for many decades. At the moment

---

[1]Most other developed countries, including America, Canada, Germany, Italy and Japan, use household survey techniques to measure employment and unemployment—sometimes in addition to a register.

the rate is calculated by dividing the wholly unemployed (or the total register) into the total number of employees, whether employed or unemployed, for the preceding June (the most accurate monthly figure of the year).

But the total number of employees (i.e., wage and salary earners) is far from representing the whole of the labour force. It excludes those who work on their own account (the self-employed), all employers, and the armed forces—about two million people altogether. If the measure is meant to show unemployment as a proportion of those in any way economically active, it should be divided into the working population.[1] The present convention not only makes the divisor (unemployment) larger than it should be; it also makes the denominator (total employees) smaller, thus exaggerating the incidence of unemployment. Table 1 demonstrates the alternatives and summarises the percentage annual rates of unemployment over the last two decades. The differences are not large, but nevertheless, in the third column, which adopts the adjustments suggested above, the unemployment percentage was never more than 2 per cent of the working population until 1968, whereas in the first column, which is the measure most frequently used, it has been 2 per cent or over more often than not since 1958.

---

[1] Even the working population is not a completely satisfactory base (Section 6).

Table 1

PERCENTAGE RATES OF UNEMPLOYMENT MEASURED BY CONVENTIONAL AND SUGGESTED METHODS, 1948 TO 1971

(Annual averages)	*Conventional Measures*		*Suggested Measure*
	Total register as % total employees	*Wholly unemployed*	*Wholly unemployed as % working popln.*
1948	1.5	—	—
1949	1.5	1.5	1.4
1950	1.5	1.5	1.4
1951	1.2	1.1	1.0
1952	2.0	1.6	1.4
1953	1.6	1.5	1.3
1954	1.3	1.2	1.1
1955	1.1	1.0	0.9
1956	1.2	1.0	0.9
1957	1.4	1.3	1.2
1958	2.1	1.9	1.7
1959	2.2	2.0	1.8
1960	1.6	1.5	1.4
1961	1.5	1.3	1.2
1962	2.0	1.8	1.7
1963	2.5	2.2	2.0
1964	1.6	1.6	1.4
1965	1.4	1.3	1.2
1966	1.5	1.4	1.3
1967	2.4	2.2	2.0
1968	2.4	2.3	2.1
1969	2.4	2.3	2.1
1970	2.6	2.5	2.3
1971	3.5	3.2	3.0

The alternative presentations for the latest possible date, 6 December, 1971, would look like this:

Total register	*Wholly unemployed as per cent of*	*Wholly unemployed*
	total employees	*working popln.*
923,000	859,000	859,000
or 4.0%	or 3.8%	or 3.5%

These adjustments, though significant, are only the beginning of the story.

15

TWO

How Long Unemployed?

The figures about unemployment discussed in Section 1 were measures at a point in time. On a certain Monday—6 December, 1971—923,000 people were registered as out of work, of whom 859,000 were wholly unemployed. But for how long had they been unemployed?

It would have been possible for many registered as out of work on 6 December to have been in work the previous Friday and back at work again in a new job the following Tuesday. The Department tries to adjust its figures for such cases, but cannot hope to do so completely. Hundreds of thousands spend a very short time on the register, finding new jobs without much difficulty.

Job mobility

Changing jobs is a desirable process both for the individual and for society. Most people want to improve their position and, in so far as moves take place from lower to higher productivity occupations, society gains. Indeed, there is no other way in which an economy can adapt itself to the future. As new tastes and new preferences develop, old jobs disappear and new ones take their place. In the process some people must leave one job to find another.[1] In so doing many may register for new work and appear as unemployed, even though they rapidly find work. Until recently about one-fifth of those on the register found work within two weeks. These people were therefore not so much without a job as between jobs.

In what sense is this 'unemployment'? Is it helpful to lump together such cases with workers who have been on the register for over six months, or even over a year, into one massive figure? The official figures most commonly quoted measure the *turnover*

---

[1] The process sometimes involves a conflict between the requirements of society for more labour mobility, to take advantage of changing patterns of demand, new techniques, etc., and the reluctance of individuals to move their place of residence or change their occupation.

of labour as well as the amount of unemployment. A proper understanding of unemployment must distinguish between the different situations.

Distinguishing the 'unemployed' from the 're-deploying'

To help towards a better understanding there seems to be a strong case for separating those out of work for short from long periods. The former ought properly to be described in some phrase which does not use the word unemployment. Even 'short-term unemployment' or 'transitional unemployment' is misleading; perhaps 're-deployment' or 'labour turnover' are better descriptions. As long as fresh jobs are available to re-absorb workers there is no reason to use the word unemployed.

To sharpen this apparent contradiction further, one might ask whether a progressive economy ought not to *prefer* a high level of labour turnover? It might well be argued that during the 1950s and early 1960s short-term 'unemployment' was too low, in the sense that the economic structure of Britain adapted itself too slowly to change. Too many companies with obsolescent products held on to their labour, thus preventing the expansion of new companies with new products. Of course, *had* the rate of change been faster, unemployment, measured as it is now, would have been so much larger, and would have caused so much concern, that policies would probably have been introduced to slow down the rate of change, and thus the rate of growth.

The amount of job changing that takes place is perhaps not fully known (and indeed is probably impossible to measure). Quarterly figures are produced by the Department of Employment which show the number of engagements in a month per 100 employees for manufacturing industries only. Between 2.0 and 3.8 engagements per 100 employees take place in a month (say, an average annual turnover of about one-third), with the rate for women (2.9 to 5.1 per month per 100) always significantly higher than that for men (1.5 to 3.5).

The proportion of these changes of job recorded in the unemployment figures is unknown, but cannot be high. If we take one-third as the annual rate of turnover, then in manufacturing industry alone, which employs about 9 million, there would be 3 million changes a year—twice the total number of recorded placements by the entire employment exchange system. Even this is probably an under-estimate. It appears that in 1970–71 no fewer than $10\frac{1}{2}$ million notifications were received by the Inland Revenue of terminations of employment (via P.45 forms).[1] Some of these

[1] 'Particulars of employee leaving' forms.

notifications may reflect double-counting of people changing jobs more than once in a year, and some are terminations of jobs by death or retirement. Nevertheless, the number of job changes in a year may still be near the 10 million mark. This makes it imperative to distinguish 'job-changing' from unemployment.

Arbitrary dividing line

Eight weeks is taken as the dividing line between 're-deployment' and 'unemployment' in this *Monograph*. The choice is arbitrary, in the sense that eight weeks in preference to six or ten has no economic significance. Some people will take longer than others to find a new job, depending probably on their level of skill. The more specialised might require more time, the unskilled less. But anyone out of work for more than two months may well be regarded as 'unemployed' rather than 'between jobs'.

Table 2 shows the number out of work for eight weeks or less as a proportion of the wholly unemployed.

Table 2

NUMBERS OUT OF WORK FOR LESS THAN EIGHT WEEKS AS PERCENTAGE OF WHOLLY UNEMPLOYED, 1948 TO 1971

	%		%
1948*	51.0	1957**	55.6
1949	50.9	1958	51.1
1950	53.7	1959	44.3
1951	56.2	1960	44.7
1952	65.4	1961	48.7
1953	53.8	1962	48.9
1954	62.2	1963	43.1
1955	63.0	1964	43.8
1956	63.6	1965	46.9
		1966	50.1
		1967	43.8
		1968	41.5
		1969	42.5
		1970	42.3
		1971	40.4

*1948–1956 at July. **1957–1971 monthly averages.
Sources: *Department of Employment Gazette; Monthly Digest of Statistics.*

In the 24 years covered by the Table, between two-fifths and two-thirds of the wholly unemployed on the day of the count found new jobs within two months. Though the proportion has recently come down, the same forces are still at work. Out of the 864,000[1] wholly unemployed on 6 December, 1971, the number out of work for less than two months was 314,500 or 36.4 per cent.

The short time between jobs for many people is, of course, the chief contrast between the situation now and before the war. Information about duration was not collected systematically until 1932, and then on a different basis. Figures quoted by Beveridge in *Full Employment in a Free Society*[2] show the contrast. Beveridge described short-term unemployment as less than six months, and pointed out that in September 1929 (according to a special inquiry) only 5 per cent of the unemployed had been out of work for more than one year, and 90 per cent for less than six months. But in 1932 the proportions had changed to 16 per cent and 70 per cent, and in 1936 to 25 per cent and 65 per cent.[3]

Importance of duration
Contemporary discussion has unfortunately overlooked completely the importance of duration in unemployment. Until 1969 hardly any reference was made to it in any of the newspapers, perhaps because it is ignored in the Department's monthly Press Notice. Even as late as 19 November, 1971, a long first leader in *The Times* headed 'Coming close to the million' did not refer to duration.[4] It is not as if the information is not easily available. For many years the Department of Employment has analysed the duration of unemployment every month, distinguishing between: those out of work for less than one week, less than two weeks and so on week by week up to eight weeks. All those out of work for more than eight weeks are then summarised in one figure. Every quarter the analysis goes into more detail and twice a year it is combined with an analysis by age.

There is therefore no difficulty in establishing the size of the 'transitional' or 're-deployment' element in some detail.

The main information about duration since 1948 is summarised in Chart 1 which shows the wholly unemployed made up from: those out of work for more than 1 year, 6 months, 2 months, 2 weeks. (The Chart will be found in the centre pages.)

---

[1]The 'duration' analysis includes school-leavers among the wholly unemployed, which some other analyses do not; hence the difference between this figure and that used earlier.

[2]George Allen and Unwin, 1944.

[3]Pre-war statistics covered a smaller proportion of the working population, as national insurance was not comprehensive.

[4]Nor is the academic debate necessarily more careful. The element of time is ignored both in the original Phillips curve (*Economica*, November 1958) and in much of its subsequent discussion.

The Chart gives a bird's eye view of the unemployment problem virtually since the end of the war. It is immediately apparent that a new situation has developed in the labour market since the end of 1966.

Before 1966 the wholly unemployed hardly ever exceeded 350,000 (the two exceptional periods, the springs of 1959 and 1963, are explained by the economic restrictions of 1958, and the exceptionally harsh winter of 1962–3 which distorted the figures for many months).

Within the ceiling of 350,000, those out of work for two months or more—again with the exceptions mentioned above—have normally been below 200,000, and for short periods below 100,000. This, on the definition advocated in this *Monograph*, would be a better measure of what really is unemployment than the figures generally used.

Numbers out of work for six months or more between 1948 and 1966 (the two exceptional periods apart), were always under 100,000, and for more than a year not often more than 50,000. These two categories comprise the so-called 'hard core' of the unemployed, to be examined more closely in Section 4.

Since 1966 the labour market has changed decisively—more people have been out of work, and for longer. Now over 400,000 are out of work for longer than two months against about 200,000 previously, and just over 100,000 for more than a year—about twice the old number.

Why this change has taken place since 1966 will be further discussed, particularly in Section 7, which examines the emergence of new kinds of unemployment.

Statistical effect of redefining unemployment

If the use of the term 'unemployment' were restricted to those out of work for more than two months, only 549,000 of the 923,000 on the total register at 6 December, 1971, would be included. Further, if these 549,000 were compared with the latest figure for the working population, then the percentage rate would be not the 4.0 generally quoted, but 2.2 per cent.

Table 3 contrasts since 1948 the total register as conventionally presented with the more careful definition of 'unemployment' measured against the working population proposed here.

The suggested measure confirms that there has been a marked increase in long-term unemployment since 1966. Before that year, only in the exceptional years 1959 and 1963 was long-term unemployment 1 per cent or over. But since 1967 long-term

Table 3

TOTAL AND LONG-TERM UNEMPLOYMENT BY CONVENTIONAL AND SUGGESTED MEASURES,. 1948 TO 1971

(*12 monthly averages*)

	Total register thousands	%*	Out of work over 8 weeks thousands	%**
1948	310.0	1.5	138.2	0.6
1949	308.0	1.5	119.2	0.5
1950	314.2	1.5	126.7	0.6
1951	252.9	1.2	81.4	0.4
1952	414.2	2.0	132.3	0.6
1953	342.0	1.6	125.9	0.5
1954	284.8	1.3	101.4	0.4
1955	232.2	1.1	77.9	0.3
1956	257.0	1.2	82.6	0.3
1957	312.5	1.4	129.3	0.5
1958	457.4	2.1	197.7	0.8
1959	475.2	2.2	243.4	1.0
1960	360.4	1.6	187.6	0.8
1961	340.7	1.5	157.1	0.6
1962	463.2	2.0	217.6	0.9
1963	573.2	2.5	291.9	1.2
1964	380.6	1.6	206.1	0.8
1965	328.8	1.4	166.1	0.6
1966	359.7	1.5	163.5	0.6
1967	559.5	2.4	290.4	1.1
1968	564.1	2.4	319.5	1.3
1969	559.3	2.4	311.1	1.2
1970	603.4	2.6	334.8	1.3
1971	806.8	3.5	450.4	1.8

*As % of total employees.   **As % of working population.

unemployment has never fallen *below* 1 per cent, and 1971 was a post-war record. Even so, in absolute terms, the numbers—300,000 to 450,000—give a very different picture from the cry of 'one million out of work'.

The rest of this *Monograph* will be largely restricted to examining the composition of long-term unemployment, the concept that really matters. Unemployment for longer than two months raises all the problems of 'structural' and 'cyclical' unemployment, as well as questions about geographical and occupational mobility.

This measure is also far more relevant to a discussion of the appropriate level of demand, even though it is by no means a measure of the additional supply of labour which a reflationary policy might bring back onto the labour market, which is considered further in Section 8.

First, however, two questions must be answered. Section 3 asks who and where the long-term unemployed are, and Section 4 questions whether they are in practice all suitable for normal employment.

THREE

Who and Where are the Long-Term Unemployed?

The analysis of the duration of unemployment produced by the Department of Employment is perhaps the most important source of information about the unemployed, and this section makes more use of it.[1] Twice a year the unemployed are analysed by age and sex as well as by duration. The duration of unemployment is shown separately for men and for women in 14 categories of time, ranging from less than a week to more than a year, for the under-eighteens, the over sixty-fives and for 10 age-groups in between.[2]

Change in the labour market since 1966

As has been explained, the rest of this *Monograph* will be primarily concerned with long-term unemployment, that is, eight weeks and over, and particular attention will be given to the change in the employment market since 1966. All the Tables in this section therefore show what has happened between July 1966 and July 1971 to the long-term unemployed—who and where they are.

The long-term unemployed increased by nearly 300,000, of whom the majority were men. Table 4 shows how this came about. It covers men and women separately, giving for each age-group the duration of their unemployment at July 1966 and July 1971.

In July 1971 there were over 100,000 men out of work for more than a year compared with under 40,000 five years previously, and a further 90,000 out of work for more than six months compared with 25,000 previously. There was a four-fold increase in those out of work between two and six months. The most substantial

---

[1] The analysis has been taken a great deal further by Mr R. F. Fowler, particularly in *Duration of Unemployment on the Register of Wholly Unemployed*, Studies in Official Statistics, Research Series No. 1, HMSO for the CSO, 1968.

[2] The information comes from the *Ministry of Labour Gazette* (August 1966, pp. 494–5, June 1967, pp. 466–9) and the *Department of Employment Gazette* (September 1971, pp. 810–14 and pp. 830–31).

Table 4

CHANGES IN LONG-TERM UNEMPLOYMENT, BY DURATION: MALES AND FEMALES, 1966 TO 1971

Duration of unemployment	Males (all ages)	
	1966	*1971*
8 to 26 weeks	43,746	176,966
26 to 52 ,,	25,225	90,268
over 52 ,,	39,094	108,033
	108,065	375,267
Increase 1966–71		*267,202*

	Females (all ages)	
8 to 26 weeks	12,972	29,884
26 to 52 ,,	5,416	11,815
over 52 ,,	5,745	9,973
	24,133	51,672
Increase 1966–71		*27,539*
Total men and women	132,198	426,939
Total increase 1966–71		*294,741*

change is the increase in those who have moved from short- to long-term unemployment.

The picture for women is quite different and on an altogether smaller scale. Only 20,000 women were registered as out of work for more than six months compared with about 10,000 at the earlier date.

To some small extent these figures include people who have retired from work, perhaps before retirement age, and although registered are unlikely to work again.[1] This element cannot be accurately measured but Table 5 gives, separately for men and for women, the increase in numbers of older people out of work. In these five years a further 80,000 older people have stayed on the

---

[1]Many who have retired prematurely remain on the register, not to get work, but to have their national insurance contributions credited, until they reach 65 (men) or 60 (women).

register. There are very few over retiring age, even now—only 1,600 men and women together.[1] This figure has barely changed over the last five years. It should be compared with the 400,000 men over 65, and more than 600,000 women over 60, who are in employment.

But compared with five years ago there are now on the register twice as many women between 50 and 60 and more than twice as many men between 55 and 65. Of the 375,000 men out of work for more than eight weeks, 125,000, or just one-third, are over 55. Nearly a quarter of the increase in long-term unemployment among men is accounted for by those approaching retiring age.

Table 5

CHANGES IN LONG-TERM UNEMPLOYMENT AMONG OLDER PEOPLE, BY AGE-GROUPS: MALES AND FEMALES, 1966 TO 1971

	Men	
Age	*1966*	*1971*
55 to 65	52,070	124,650
over 65	986	1,253
	53,056	125,903
Increase 1966–71		72,847
	Women	
50 to 60	7,232	14,228
60 and over	296	374
	7,528	14,602
Increase 1966–71		7,074
Total men and women:	60,584	140,505
Total increase 1966–71		79,921

The pattern of long-term unemployment

In so far as the statistics are any guide at all, female long-term unemployment is still not much of a problem. To some extent this reflects the fact that when women lose their jobs or withdraw from work, particularly married women, they either do not bother or have

---

[1] Men aged over 65 and women over 60.

no incentive to register.[1] As fewer than 30,000 of the increase of 300,000 out of work in the last five years under review were women, the rest of this section examines the position for men only. An analysis by age and by region is possible, taking two age-groups, between 20 and 40, and over 40. The results are striking.

Nationally, the figures show that between 1966 and 1971 the increase in unemployment among the 40 and over group was three-fold, and between 20 and 40 five-fold.[2] In July 1971, 2.2 per cent of males between 20 and 40 had been out of work for more than eight weeks compared with 0.4 per cent five years earlier. For older men the percentage had risen from 1.1 to 3.0. With figures like these we need not doubt that there has been an increase in real unemployment. We are not dealing here with any of the 'fringe' areas of the labour force—students, married women, or the unemployable. Most of these men after all have recently been in regular work (though they may to some extent have been 'hoarded' labour).

Table 6

LONG-TERM UNEMPLOYMENT, BY REGIONS, MEN OVER 40, AS PERCENTAGE OF EMPLOYEES, 1966 TO 1971

	1966	*1971*	*1966*	*1971*
	Number		*%*	
Great Britain	80,733	218,513	1.1	3.0
Scotland	14,839	31,731	2.2	4.8
London and South East	11,138	27,636	0.4	1.1
North West	10,491	28,852	1.1	3.2
Northern	9,326	23,662	2.1	5.4
Midlands	7,675	33,966	0.6	2.8
Eastern and Southern	7,534	21,180	0.4	1.0
Wales	7,187	13,348	2.1	4.2
South-West	6,918	14,140	1.5	3.2
Yorkshire—Humberside	5,625	24,098	0.8	3.7

[1]The statistics may therefore fail to record many women who do want work (Section 6).

[2]The figures are derived from the duration analysis by age-groups and by regions taken together with the annual analysis of employees in Great Britain. The latter analyses the number of employees by region and by age. The percentage used therefore has to be the numbers of unemployed adult males compared with the number of *employees,* which (Section 1) is less than the total working population, and smaller still than the potential labour force.

The regional pattern of long-term unemployment among adult men is particularly interesting. Table 6 gives information about men over 40, which inevitably includes some retired people.

In 1966 unemployment among adult males aged 40 and over was less than 1 per cent throughout the country except in Scotland, Wales, the North East, the South West and marginally the North West. Elsewhere, unemployment was very low. In London and the South East, for instance, there were only 11,000 men over 40 out of work for more than two months, compared with well over 2 million employees.

The change in 1971 has been sharp. Only in the Eastern and Southern Region and the London and South-East Region is unemployment at or near 1 per cent. Even in the Midlands it is just under 3 per cent and in Scotland and the Northern Region either side of 5 per cent. That is to say that in the last two areas, with a labour force of approximately 2 million, about 5 per cent of men over the age of 40 have been out of work for more than two months. In Yorkshire—Humberside the change has been dramatic, from 0.8 per cent to 3.7 per cent unemployment.

Rise in unemployment among younger men

This is striking enough, but perhaps what has happened in the younger age-group, shown in Table 7, is even more remarkable.

In 1966 only 0.4 per cent of men between 20 and 40 were out of work for more than two months throughout Great Britain. The

Table 7
LONG-TERM UNEMPLOYMENT, BY REGIONS, MEN AGED 20–40, AS PERCENTAGE OF EMPLOYEES, 1966 TO 1971

	1966	1971	1966	1971
	Number		%	
Great Britain	24,099	132,655	0.4	2.2
Scotland	6,500	27,791	1.2	5.1
London and South East	3,039	13,516	0.1	0.7
North West	3,507	22,900	0.5	3.1
Northern	2,939	13,715	0.9	4.0
Midlands	1,972	18,837	0.2	1.6
Eastern and Southern	1,294	9,109	0.8	5.3
Wales	2,317	7,420	0.9	2.8
South West	1,169	5,419	0.3	1.6
Yorkshire—Humberside	1,352	14,218	0.2	2.7

27

absolute figure, 24,000, must be compared with the relevant labour force of nearly 6 million. Only in Scotland was unemployment in this age-group over 1 per cent, and even there the absolute figure— 6,500—was far smaller than the labour force in many companies. The change has been dramatic. Unemployment in July 1966 was at 5 per cent or more in Scotland and the Eastern and Southern Region, 4 per cent in the North and below 1 per cent only in London and the South East. Again it should be repeated that these figures and percentages refer only to men between 20 and 40 out of work for more than eight weeks.

Although it is true that some now on the general unemployment register are unemployable, those who have recently been in work and who have come on to the register only in the last five years are unlikely to fall into that category.

The position may be summarised thus. As far as the figures are any guide, long-term female unemployment hardly exists. The increase in women out of work for more than six months has been slight—about 10,000 between 1966 and 1971, of whom the bulk were older women. Indeed, of the 9,973 women recorded as out of work for more than one year at 12 July, 1971, 5,311, or 53.2 per cent, were over 55. Of the 9,973 women noted as out of work for more than a year, 5,595, or 56.1 per cent, lived in Scotland, Wales, the Northern and North Western regions of Britain.

Long-term adult male unemployment trebled between 1966 and 1971. The regional distribution by age is similar to that for women. Of the 108,053 men out of work for more than a year, 56,347, or 52.2 per cent, lived in the four development regions mentioned above and 58,061, or 53.7 per cent, were more than 55 years old.

Failure of regional employment policies

The various regional policies of successive post-war administrations seem to have done little to change the pattern of unemployment. Well over half of the long-term unemployed continue to live in these areas. Though a full study of this problem is beyond the scope of this *Monograph*, there seems to be little evidence that the regional rates of unemployment are in any way converging to the national average.[1] Scotland and the Northern Region continue to be substantially above the average, with London, the South East and the Midlands well below. Such slight evidence of a reduction in the deviation from the average seems to have been as much due

---

[1]The Under Secretary of State for Employment, in reply to a question in the House as recently as 3 February, 1972, said 'Certainly the regional disparity remains as it was before'.

to the growth in unemployment in the formerly prosperous regions as to improvement in the areas of high unemployment. An extensive study would be required to test this hypothesis.

Unfortunately it is not possible to complement this analysis of regional unemployment by age and sex with an analysis of long-term unemployment by occupation. The duration analyses of the Department of Employment do not include such information. But there is plenty of material to show in some detail the occupations of those on the unemployment register every month on the day of the count. Over half the men unemployed are labourers, and nearly half the women are factory hands, charwomen and other unskilled workers.

FOUR

The Unemployables

Even when the pressure of demand has been most intense, and indeed unsustainable, as in 1951, 1955 and 1966, many people were still 'unemployed'. If they were unable to find work in those years, will they ever be able to do so? What sort of people can they be? Are they perhaps physically impaired, mentally handicapped, or work-shy? This section analyses the 'unemployables', who make up what is frequently called the 'hard core' of unemployment.[1]

How many 'hard-core' unemployed?

A convention seems to have developed for putting a figure of about 200,000 on the 'hard core'. In the debate in the House of Commons on 9 November, 1971, Mr Roy Jenkins, Chancellor of the Exchequer in the last Labour Government, even referred to 'an irreducible minimum' of 250,000 unemployed which 'we can never hope to approach'. It seems almost certain, however, that he was referring to both short- and long-term unemployment, and this ambiguity merely confirms how important it is to distinguish between the two.[2]

One would expect the bulk of the hard core of unemployables to be included in the figure of long-term unemployment, but not to exceed it. But, as is clear from Table 3 (page 21), if the hard core of unemployed really amounts to 200,000, then for most of the post-war period we must have had 'negative' unemployment, which is absurd, with real unemployment emerging only in 1959, 1962–4, and since 1967.

Part of the difficulty is due to the concept of the 'hard core', which is an unhappy one for the economist. As Chart 1 (centre pages) makes plain, there is not, and never has been, a fixed or absolute amount of unemployment. As the total rises or falls, a corresponding

---

[1]The discussion is about the physically unemployable, not the economically unemployable, though the distinction is far from absolute.

[2]There is a short discussion of the evidence on the numbers of 'unemployables' in Professor F. W. Paish's *Policy for Incomes*, Hobart Paper 29, IEA, 1964 (Fourth Edition, 1968), pp. 28–29.

change can be noted throughout all the 'strata' of unemployment, though the original impact has been cushioned by the time it reaches the very long-term unemployed. The total out of work for more than six months has sometimes been lower than 50,000, and even before 1966 had also exceeded 100,000. The 'hard core' evidently has soft edges.

Nearly everyone in the non-institutional population can be usefully employed at some wage. When labour is particularly scarce, with prices and profits rising, it pays employers to take on progressively less suitable workers. Labour is not homogeneous, and some workers are not worth employing, except in time of peak demand. Then their marginal product is positive, but only as long as the level of demand necessary to bring them into employment can be maintained.

We come to a type of unemployment which has been neglected since the days of the classical economists—unsuitability for work. This is quite different from the standard categories of transitional, cyclical, and structural unemployment—all of which are, so to speak, on the demand side, and disregard problems about the quality of the supply of labour.

Distinguishing the 'unemployables'

It must be important to distinguish between people who are not fit for normal and regular employment, and those who are. There is a strong case on social and economic grounds for recording the former separately from the unemployment register. They will probably be people who require the care and attention of the social services, rather than simply 'work', and a separate register may help to identify them.

From the economic point of view, unless such people are excluded, they will prevent the attainment of anything like 'full' employment or zero (long-term) unemployment. Their presence on the register also lends spurious support to the view that the economy needs to be reflated in order to reduce unemployment. But unemployment due to complete unsuitability for work will never be reduced by any amount of reflation, and to try to do so damages the whole economy.

It is difficult to estimate how many people may be unsuitable for normal work, since neither 'suitability' nor 'normal work' can be defined. There are only three sources of information, which are not entirely reconcilable. The Department of Employment is charged under the Disabled Persons (Employment) Acts, 1944 and 1958, with keeping a Register of Disabled Persons to help them find either normal or sheltered employment. Some regular figures are available from this register.

31

A recent inquiry by the Social Survey Division of the Office of Population Censuses into the *Handicapped and Impaired in Great Britain* provides a little information about the employment and unemployment of such people, but it is incidental to the main purpose of the survey, which was in any case a once-for-all inquiry.[1]

The most direct information, now unfortunately out of date, comes from two *ad hoc* inquiries in 1961 and 1964, by the then Ministry of Labour, into the 'characteristics' of the unemployed.

From all this information it is still not possible to say with much accuracy how many people now unemployed are unsuitable for normal work. It may be that something like 150,000 of those now included among the *long-term* unemployed are unlikely to be able to undertake normal and regular work.

Reserve of labour?

Both the surveys from the Ministry of Labour took place when there was general preoccupation with the 'manpower shortage' and they were partly designed to see whether there was a 'reserve' of unused labour among the unemployed. The first analysed the 219,000 wholly unemployed adults claiming unemployment benefit, the second 313,000 wholly unemployed adults, some of whom were not claiming benefit. In all important respects the second inquiry confirmed the first. Both took place at times of very low unemployment—on the conventional measure 1.4 per cent in August 1961 and 1.5 per cent in October 1964 (the alternative measure proposed in this *Monograph* for these years was 0.6 and 0.8 per cent—Table 3). That unemployment was exceptionally low makes the findings of the survey all the more interesting. For it was quite clear that very few—perhaps 30,000 to 50,000—could be regarded in any way as 'available' for work, and then only in the special sense that they were classified as capable of working, but as the *local* opportunities open to them were limited, and they were not prepared to move, they remained unemployed.

Both surveys found that a substantial proportion (73,000 out of 313,000 second inquiry, 43,000 out of 219,000 first inquiry) on the register would get work without delay and were indeed in process

---

[1]Inquiry by the Office of Population Censuses and Surveys, Social Survey Division, *Work and Housing of Impaired Persons in Great Britain,* by Judith R. Buckle: Part II of an inquiry carried out on behalf of the Department of Health and Social Security, the Scottish Home and Health Department, the Welsh Office—in conjunction with other Government Departments, HMSO, 1971.

of doing so. This is a further insight into the importance of the high turnover of labour discussed in Section 2. Only 36,000 in the first and 54,000 in the second inquiry were categorised as finding work difficult to get *only* because of the lack of local opportunities. This was the extent of the reserve of labour in the sense of people perfectly capable of working who would do so only if work were brought to them and made available in their area. Most of them were married women.

For the remainder there was little hope of work for various kinds of personal reasons. In the second survey 63,000 were difficult to place because of age. 50,000 of these older people had been out of work for more than six months and three-quarters of them were in the development areas. 60,000 suffered from some mental or physical condition which limited their scope for employment—again about three-quarters of them were in the development areas.

The next most important category was 30,000 whose 'attitude to work' made them difficult to place, of whom just under 5,000 were classified as difficult to place on grounds of colour, inability to speak English and lack of union membership. 4,000 were recorded as lacking financial incentive to work; it is not clear whether these claimed or did not claim unemployment benefit. Just over 9,000, largely married women, were difficult to place because they were available only at hours of their own choosing.

So 180,000 people, or nearly three-fifths of the recorded 'unemployed', were thus, as the survey commented, 'likely to spend long periods on the register even when local demand for labour is high'. This is the 'hard core' and is in the main unskilled, elderly and disabled and unable to profit by rehabilitation or training. A figure of 200,000 for the current position may not be far out.

Should these people be on the register at all? The survey says 'it seems clear that this group will remain a feature of the labour market', but they are not really part of the market. Further, 'all the services of the Ministry are deployed to help them, as individuals, to find jobs', but this is clearly a task for which the employment exchange service may not be well equipped. Ought the responsibility to rest with the Department of Employment? Would it not be better to record these people separately and to make them the responsibility of the Department of Health and Social Security?[1]

---

[1]The following paragraph appears in the 1969 Annual Report of the Department of Health and Social Security:

'During the year work continued on the development of a questionnaire for use in those cases where unemployment appears to have continued unduly

(continued on p.34)

Register of disabled persons

These Ministry of Labour surveys each made a brief reference to the registered disabled. The first survey found that about 20 per cent of the wholly unemployed were registered as disabled persons, less than half of whom were considered good placement propositions. It also found that of the men regarded as difficult to place because of age or physical condition, the latter 'was by no means confined to the registered disabled'. Evidently many registered as unemployed may be disabled, but not registered as such.

Over 600,000 people are on the official disabled register—the figure has come down from just over 700,000 in 1960. The overwhelming majority were in employment (normal or sheltered). Even in November 1971, when unemployment was high, only 68,000 disabled men and 8,000 disabled women suitable for ordinary employment were on the register but out of work. In addition about 12,000 registered disabled were so severely handicapped that they were unlikely to be able to work except under special conditions. These 12,000 are excluded from all figures of employment and unemployment.

Whether the disabled register is comprehensive or not is a separate study, but the reference in the Ministry of Labour survey suggests that it may not be, and this inference seems to be confirmed by information in the Social Survey on Impaired People.

The Social Survey estimated that 'the number of impaired people in the labour force at the time of the inquiry which took place at the end of 1968 and the beginning of 1969 was 697,000'. This is slightly higher than the number of 646,000 on the Disabled Persons Register at April 1969, but too much should not be made of this similarity, as the definitions of disablement and impairment are substantially different. [1] Nevertheless, there is a further coincidence

---

long in spite of the controls described. The object is to investigate in depth the underlying reasons for the unemployment, bearing in mind that in times of high unemployment there must always be some men who are on the borderline of employability and who in competition with other men will fail to obtain what work is available. The problem is to identify and help, e.g., by re-establishment courses, those who are capable of benefiting from such courses or who require medical or psychological treatment.' (p. 98)

Unfortunately, no progress was made with this project, partly because of the pressure of work on local offices. It is to be hoped that the project will be revived as soon as possible, and once again, by concentrating on those out of work for, say, a year, the number of cases to be investigated could be cut down sufficiently drastically to make the project manageable.

[1] A disabled person is one who 'is substantially handicapped in obtaining or keeping employment', and diseases of the heart, lungs, nervous and mental

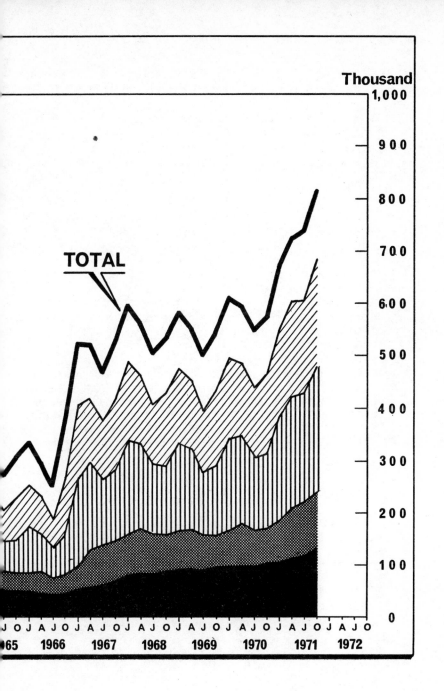

really are unfit for normal work, then it looks as if the economy in the past was often run at 'zero' or even 'negative' unemployment, which is ridiculous. The answer is that this 200,000 does not consist of the same men and women who remain permanently out of work. Rather it records that, at any moment of time, there are 200,000 difficult cases to place, many of whom may have been in employment for a short while, but failed to remain at work. The first Ministry of Labour survey of the characteristics of the unemployed showed that men who had been out of work longest also had the worst employment record in previous years. To some extent, therefore, as they move frequently in and out of employment, they will also show up in the statistics of labour turnover as short-term unemployed. That is why it is incorrect to allot the whole 200,000 to long-term unemployment. A proportion, say, 50,000, will at any moment be recorded as short-term unemployed.

This adjustment helps to resolve the absurdity of 'negative' unemployment. But even if only 150,000 of the long-term unemployed were assumed to be unemployable, there is still a difficulty. No allowance has yet been made for such 'structural' or 'cyclical' unemployment as must have existed. If we guess a figure of about 50,000 for unemployment of this kind, and add to it the 150,000 specified above, then only since 1967 has there been any real long-term unemployment, which has been very low in absolute figures— a matter of 100,000 to 150,000.

Can this really be the measure of those who might have been brought back into employment if effective demand had been higher in those years? As far as the figures go, this seems to be so. But the statistics are far from covering the whole story of unemployment or, more importantly, employment (Section 6).

FIVE

Other Indicators in the Employment Market

Unemployment is only one indicator of changes in demand and supply in the labour market. Other measures include the number of hours worked, overtime and short-time, length of holidays, and, on the demand side, outstanding vacancies. As pressure in the labour market varies, so these other indicators ought to change in the direction which corroborates recorded movements in employment and unemployment. And the balance of all forces at work should be reflected in changes in the price of labour services, whether measured by wage-rates or earnings.

In practice only one indicator—that of vacancies—seems as yet to confirm unequivocally the transformation of the labour market suggested by the figures of unemployment.

Vacancies as an economic indicator

Comparison is frequently made between the number of vacancies notified by employers to the employment exchanges and the number of unemployed. There is something to be said for this comparison, subject to the major reservation that notified vacancies cover only a very small part of the spectrum of skills and occupations. The employment exchanges are traditionally thought of as finding work for manual workers, the semi-skilled and unskilled, and most markets for other types of labour (e.g., secretaries, doctors) function without any contact at all with them, or even with the specialist services for professional and scientific employment, nursing, catering and office work.

The Department has estimated that its 1,000 employment exchanges placed about $1\frac{1}{2}$ million adults in new (largely manual) jobs each year, perhaps one-fifth of all engagements.[1] Clearly the state exchanges are less important in making a market for labour than alternative channels such as newspaper advertisements,

---

[1] Department of Employment, *Future of the Employment Service*, Consultative Document, July 1970.

private agencies and personal contact, but from none of these channels are any statistics available.[1]

As the Introductory Notes to *British Labour Statistics—Historical Abstract* conclude, statistics of vacancies

'exclude all those vacancies which were not notified to these offices. Thus they do not purport to measure the total extent to which employers' immediate manpower requirements remain unsatisfied. Nevertheless experience has shown that the changes in the series of statistics of vacancies for adults reflect changes in the pressure of demand in the labour market'.

Vacancies may indicate changes in the pressure, but they cannot indicate the absolute level of demand.

The public discussion again fails to distinguish between men and women, and makes no allowance for the duration of unemployment. It is not only that the larger part—perhaps 80 per cent—of people recorded as unemployed change jobs quite successfully without the help of a labour exchange; time must also be allowed for the exchanges to match vacancies with placings.

Table 8 compares the figures of outstanding vacancies with those out of work for more than eight weeks, separately for adult men and adult women. The Table again emphasises how different these two labour markets are.

Since 1958 there have been more vacancies for women than women available (i.e., on the unemployment register). In 1966, for every woman out of work over two months there were nearly four vacancies recorded. In 1971, for the first time, there were roughly the same number of vacancies as women registering themselves as available.

The male labour market shows a very different pattern. Here there have nearly always been more men available than vacancies for them. From 1960 to 1961 and 1964 to 1966 there was a rough balance. But in other years, notably 1963, and increasingly since 1967, vacancies have not grown at anything like the same rate as long-term unemployment. In 1971 there were fewer vacancies available than ever, and for each nearly six men were available.

Dealing in annual figures for the whole country is, of course, a very crude way of analysing the problem. Nevertheless, the changes which have taken place, particularly in 1971, are significant, and more detailed information is available enabling vacancies to be analysed by area and by occupation. At the latest available date—1 December, 1971—of 60,000 vacancies notified for adult

---

[1]On all this Christina Fulop's *Markets for Employment*, Research Monograph 26, IEA, 1971, is enlightening, especially Section 3.

Table 8

ADULT VACANCIES AS A RATIO OF LONG-TERM UNEMPLOYMENT, 1958 TO 1971

(Monthly averages, thousands)

	MEN			WOMEN	
	Out of work	Vacancies	Men to vacancies	Out of work	Vacancies	Vacancies to women
1958	147.9	—	—	49.8	—	—
1959	183.5	88.2	2.08	59.9	68.7	1.15
1960	141.5	121.0	1.17	46.1	90.9	1.97
1961	119.6	123.9	0.96	37.5	89.4	2.38
1962	169.0	77.8	2.17	48.6	71.7	1.47
1963	228.7	70.7	3.23	63.2	73.7	1.16
1964	161.3	114.6	1.15	44.8	106.2	2.37
1965	131.3	143.4	0.92	34.8	121.7	3.50
1966	133.1	137.5	0.97	30.4	117.3	3.86
1967	241.9	92.0	2.63	48.5	82.1	1.69
1968	276.0	92.6	2.98	43.5	95.4	2.19
1969	273.1	102.8	2.66	38.0	96.7	2.54
1970	294.4	100.7	2.92	40.4	85.1	2.11
1971	392.7	69.0	5.69	57.7	60.0	1.04

Sources: *British Labour Statistics: Historical Abstract;*
Department of Employment Gazette;
Monthly Digest of Statistics.

men, nearly half—27,000—were in the South East. Of these 60,000 jobs, just under one-third were in the manufacturing industries, and rather over one-third in services of all kinds, including distribution, transport, insurance and banking.

In spite of all qualifications more use could be made of the figures for vacancies, particularly when distinguished between men and women, as an indicator. Chart 2 shows vacancies open to adult males in January, April, July and October of the last seven years, compared with the amount of adult male long-term unemployment. The beginning of the developments which have led to heavy unemployment at the end of 1971 can be quite clearly seen in the divergent trend since the end of 1966.

The Chart presents a sharper picture than the more familiar comparison of vacancies and unemployment, which does not allow for duration or distinguish by sex.

Other indicators

In contrast to the figures for vacancies, particularly those for adult males, other trends in the labour market have not behaved as might

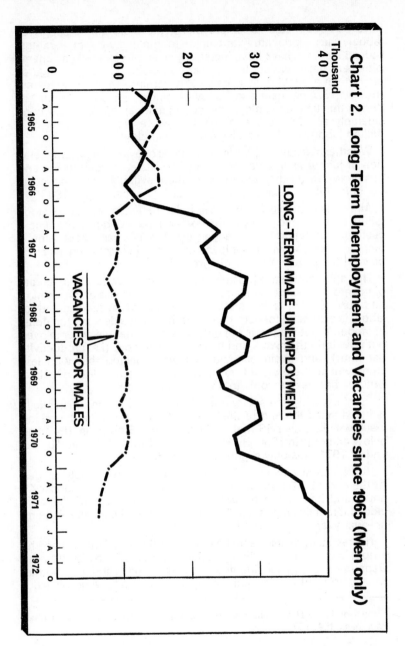

Chart 2. Long-Term Unemployment and Vacancies since 1965 (Men only)

have been expected. Unemployment (the more ample supply of labour) has made little difference to the increase in earnings. Indeed incomes have been increasing even more rapidly as unemployment has gone up. In the year to October 1970 (later figures are not yet available), average weekly earnings of manual workers rose by 13.7 per cent and hourly earnings by 15.4 per cent. Yet during this time unemployment among manual workers grew considerably and by October 1970 there were nearly a quarter of a million labourers alone registered as unemployed.

Whether measured by basic wage-rates or by earnings, remuneration of labour as a factor of production has continued to rise and has grown faster than output, with the inevitable result that costs per unit of output have risen by about 50 per cent since 1963.

All this is generally known, and indeed reflects the conspicuous failure of economic policy in the post-war period, but to the almost customary inflation is now added the new and remarkable simultaneous increase in unemployment. Why this is taking place is beyond the scope of this *Monograph.* [1]

This apparently strong demand for labour, as reflected in its rate of reward, is to some extent confirmed by an analysis of information on hours of work. It is sometimes overlooked that the demand for labour is a demand for performance rather than a demand for 'units' of labour. What matters is not only how many people are employed but how long they work and how well they work (i.e. productivity per hour), and again one would have expected that with less employment there would be more short-time and less overtime. But this has been so only to a very limited extent.

Normal weekly hours throughout industry have been substantially reduced since the end of the war. In 1946 the standard working week was just over 46 hours. It fell below 45 hours in 1947 and below 44 hours in 1960. By 1966 it was below 41 hours and by the end of 1971 was only slightly above 40 hours.

Hours actually worked, however, are still considerably longer. At the end of 1970 the average working week was just under 45 hours and had changed hardly at all since the end of the war; indeed it remains not much shorter than the working week in many pre-war years.

The result, of course, is that a considerable part of many workers' output is paid for at overtime rates. In the industries covered by the Department's regular inquiries into average earnings, normal weekly hours of 40.1 are paid for by normal weekly wage-rates but

[1]Professor F. A. Hayek offers explanations in *A Tiger by the Tail*, Hobart Paperback, IEA, 1972.

an extra 4.5 hours have to be paid for at overtime rates of time and a quarter, time and a half, and perhaps more.

In order to bring down costs at a time of relatively high unemployment, employers might be expected to reduce the amount of overtime they had to pay by employing *more* people for a normal working week in preference to fewer people with regular overtime.

Table 9 shows what has happened in manufacturing industries only and also gives the available information on short-time.

Overtime a deep-rooted tradition?

The main points may be stated quite briefly. There is still very little short-time working. The figures, which are for a single week in mid-year, normally June, show that 69,000 operatives had been put on short-time in June 1971 with a total loss of 753,000 hours. Even the latest figure available, for the week ending 11 December, is not large. Just under 2 per cent of operatives were affected, under $1\frac{1}{4}$ million hours lost. This was rather higher than in the previous few years but by no means unusual. In 1952 over 5 million hours were lost by short-time working, largely due to difficulties in the Lancashire textile industry.

The overtime situation is quite different and unexpected. Overtime has for years been a regular characteristic of work in most manufacturing industries. Between one-fifth and one-third of workers are regularly on overtime and do between $7\frac{1}{2}$ and $8\frac{1}{2}$ hours per week. The amount of overtime being worked in the week ended 19 June, 1971, though lower than for many years, was not exceptionally low. Just over 30 per cent of those in manufacturing industries, or 1.7 million workers, worked an average of 8 hours overtime each, which is the equivalent of over 14 million extra hours per week.

These figures are worth some attention. The Table shows that more work is now done on overtime than in earlier years—which reflects, of course, the cut in the number of normal working hours. In the mid-sixties almost twice as much overtime was worked as in the early fifties.

From the beginning of June 1965 until the end of 1971 the minimum amount of overtime worked in any week was 14.6 million hours (January 1967), and the maximum was 19.54 million hours (13 December, 1969). These are remarkable figures if converted into the number of extra people who would be needed if—for argument's sake—overtime work were to be banned. On the assumption of a 40-hour week it would require 486,000 extra people to make up the overtime worked on the larger figure and 366,000 on the smaller. Both figures exceed the numbers of long-term unemployed recorded at those dates.

During 1971, however, a new trend developed as the amount of overtime declined. Since the week ended 19 June, overtime hours dropped from 14 million to just over 13½ million, the lowest figure since 1959 but still substantial.

Table 9
OVERTIME AND SHORT-TIME WORKED IN MANUFACTURING INDUSTRY, 1950 TO 1971

	OVERTIME				SHORT-TIME		
	No. of workers on overtime (thousands)	% of all workers	Average hours overtime per worker	Number of overtime hours worked (millions)	No. of workers on short-time (thousands)	% of all workers	Total hours lost (thousands)
1950*	1,050	—	8	8.0	37	—	471
1951	1,254	21.6	8	9.9	35	0.6	418
1952	1,159	20.7	7½	8.9	304	5.4	5,186
1953	1,306	23.7	8	10.2	62	1.1	676
1954	1,498	26.5	8	12.1	41	0.7	438
1955	1,577	26.5	8	12.4	59	1.0	808
1956	1,540	25.9	8	12.1	99	1.7	1,105
1957	1,509	26.3	8	11.9	63	1.1	640
1958	1,293	22.4	7½	9.8	217	3.8	3,000
1959	1,461	25.7	7½	11.0	82	1.4	1,068
1960	1,773	31.4	8	14.0	31	0.5	303
1961	1,982	31.9	8	15.88	42	0.7	520
1962	1,770	28.8	8	13.82	89	1.4	994
1963	1,749	29.4	8	13.83	68	1.1	750
1964	2,064	34.0	8½	17.20	29	0.5	298
1965	2,113	34.9	8½	17.88	25	0.4	274
1966	2,199	35.5	8½	18.73	29	0.5	249
1967	1,939	33.0	8½	16.26	94	1.6	1,041
1968	2,045	35.3	8½	17.19	30	0.5	305
1969	2,171	36.5	8½	18.91	29	0.5	403
1970	2,086	35.3	8½	17.80	32	0.5	413
1971	1,731	30.7	8	14.19	70	1.2	760
1971 Dec.	1,674	30.3	8	13.62	105	1.9	1,245

*Figures are for one week in June of each year.
Sources: *British Labour Statistics: Year Book 1969; Gazette.*

These figures for overtime are limited to manufacturing industries, and within those industries to operatives. The numbers covered seem to be about six million, or less than a quarter of the working population. No information is available about overtime worked in other parts of the economy, but it must be considerable, perhaps as much again.

It seems that there remains a strong demand for the services of labour in many parts of the economy even when there is unemployment elsewhere. Employers are unable to reduce overtime in order to keep down costs. The labour market is not working properly if labour fails to move into areas, industries and occupations where most needed. Such lack of mobility—partly due to the lack of houses to rent, partly to unwillingness to change place of residence—may well be more important as a *cause* of unemployment than inadequate demand.

SIX

A Hidden Workforce ?

Less than half the total population, and less than two-thirds of the population over 15, is in the labour force. What the remaining one-third comprises, and what the approximately 15 million people in it are doing, determines whether or not there is a 'hidden reserve' of labour, and therefore, as some observers believe, substantial unrecorded unemployment.

Data available from the Department of Employment derives from people either being in employment or registering that they are not. All who fail to register, for whatever reason, will not be counted as unemployed and will be outside the scope of any figures compiled by the Department. They are simply treated as if they have left the labour force.

Shrinking labour force

That is what appears to have been happening on a dramatic scale since 1966. The working population grew steadily year by year (with a slight set-back in 1958) from the end of the war until the autumn of 1966. But for the last five years it has been falling. Between September 1966 and June 1971 it fell by more than 860,000 workers. Since the wholly unemployed increased by 363,000, there were nearly $1\frac{1}{4}$ million fewer people at work.[1]

This reduction almost certainly continued throughout the second half of 1971 and into the spring of 1972. The number of wholly unemployed increased by nearly 200,000 between June 1971 and January 1972, and if the fall in the working population has continued at the same rate as in 1970–71 a further loss of over 100,000 workers will be recorded when more up-to-date figures become available. It seems probable that the recorded working population has shrunk by over a million since September 1966, and together

---

[1] The wholly unemployed are, of course, counted as part of the 'working' population. Students of the subject have to accustom themselves to the nomenclature which insists that a man may be in the working population but not working, an employee without employment, and part of the occupied population but without a job.

with the increase in the wholly unemployed there are at least $1\frac{1}{2}$ million fewer men and women in employment.

Decline in male employees

Once again the details of the fall in the working population are more revealing than the aggregate figures. Table 10 shows how the composition of the working population has changed during the last decade and how unemployment has varied for men and for women. Unemployment is measured both by 'wholly unemployed' and by long-term (over eight weeks) unemployment.

The employment of female labour has altered little. The female working population has varied since 1962 between 8,540,000 and 9,030,000; although now lower than in previous years, it is not significantly so. Long-term unemployment among women is small, swinging 20,000 either side of a figure of 40,000—a very low absolute level. At June 1971, long-term unemployment for adult women was 0.6 per cent of the female working population, most of which was among older women and in the development areas. The outstanding feature is that the female working population remains larger than it was in the first half of the sixties, though slightly smaller than in the peak years of 1969 and 1970.

This situation is not true for men. The male working population in June 1971 was more than three-quarters of a million below the peak of 16,654,000 reached in December 1965. This is a much more important statistic about the male labour market than the increase of 250,000 in long-term unemployment among adult males between mid-1965 and mid-1971. Taking men and women together, the reduction in the working population has been four times as large as the increase in long-term unemployment, but it has not provoked anything like the same attention.

For the last five years the working population has clearly formed a shrinking proportion of the population, whether measured against the population over 15 or, better still, the population of working age (men 15 to 64, women 15 to 59).

		1966 (thousands)	1971 (thousands)
Population over 15	(June)	40,866.6	41,244.8*
Population of working age	(June)	32,747.2	32,609.0*
Working population	(Sept.) 25,695.0	(June) 24,827.0
Working population as % of population over 15		62.9	60.2
Working population as % of population of working age		78.5	76.1

*1970 figures.

Table 10

WORKING POPULATION AND UNEMPLOYMENT: MALES AND FEMALES, 1962 TO 1971

(Thousands)

	Male Working Population	Wholly Unemployed Adult Males		Female Working Population	Wholly Unemployed Adult Females	
		total	over 8 weeks		total	over 8 weeks
1962*	16,507	278	154	8,539	95	43
1963	16,548	346	214	8,590	115	60
1964	16,546	240	147	8,722	77	41
1965	16,604	207	120	8,859	63	31
1966	16,556	199	112	9,027	54	25
1967	16,457	378	277	8,935	88	45
1968	16,285	429	268	8,948	77	40
1969	16,191	415	258	9,016	68	34
1970	16,023	450	281	9,021	73	37
1971	15,867	589	370	8,960	98	50

*At June each year.
Source: Department of Employment Gazette.

A shrinking total labour force puts changes in recorded unemployment into a different perspective. We appear to be engaged in the extraordinary practice of carefully recording as 'unemployed' up to 400,000 who are between jobs and 200,000 who may be unemployable, while ignoring the loss of about a million workers who are probably fit, willing to work, and until recently have been working. For this reason the working population does not provide the perfect denominator for the unemployment percentage (page 14).

'Activity rates'

Table 11 further confirms this fall in the male working population by showing 'activity rates' by age-groups for men from 1966 to 1969 and for women from 1966 to 1970.[1] These 'activity rates' measure the proportion of employees in each age/sex group who were 'economically active', against the total population in such groups. The male activity rate has fallen from 76.7 per cent in 1966 to 73.5 per cent in 1969. The decline occurred in each age-group, even among men aged 25 to 44, where a high rate of participation would be expected.

There was a slight decline in the activity rate of females—from 40.5 per cent to 40.1 per cent between 1966 and 1970—largely because fewer women under 24 were at work. More women from 25 to 44 and from 45 to 59 became employed, in contrast to men in those age-groups.

The regional analysis shows that in the younger 'adult' group the activity rate among men has *fallen* in every region, but for women of similar age it has *increased* everywhere except in the West Midlands. Among older adults the male activity rate has fallen in seven out of the 11 regions, in contrast to the increase shown for women in every region in the roughly similar age-group.

Women replacing men?

It seems that the substitution of women for men (which has been taking place for two decades) continues to be important. The relative lack of unionisation among women is probably one reason for their larger employment opportunities, which only equal pay can now spoil.

The substitution of women for men, however, is not on a sufficient scale to explain the fall in the male labour force. Nor is the fall to be

---

[1]Unfortunately, the Department of Employment has decided to discontinue providing this information for men, simply because it was considered to give an insufficiently useful comparison region by region. But as the figures throw light on the national decline in total adult male employees it is to be hoped that this decision will be reconsidered.

Table 11
ANNUAL EMPLOYEE ACTIVITY RATES: MALES 1966 TO 1969, FEMALES 1966 TO 1970
(Per cent)

	South East England*	South East	East Anglia	South Western	West Midlands	East Midlands	Yorks and Humberside	North Western	Northern	Wales	Scotland	Great Britain
Males and females												
Aged 15 and over												
1966	60.0	60.9	49.9	48.2	62.8	57.0	58.3	59.4	53.3	48.4	57.0	57.8
1967	59.1	60.1	49.1	47.4	61.1	57.6	56.6	58.5	52.6	47.3	56.7	56.9
1968	58.8	59.7	48.5	47.0	60.2	56.3	56.1	58.1	51.8	47.1	56.4	56.4
1969	58.3	59.1	49.9	46.5	59.5	55.9	56.0	57.9	51.8	46.7	56.6	56.1
Males												
Aged 15 and over												
1966	78.7	79.8	67.1	65.7	82.4	75.4	78.1	77.8	73.3	68.2	75.9	76.7
1967	77.5	78.6	65.8	64.5	80.1	76.0	75.9	76.8	72.1	66.7	75.5	75.5
1968	76.7	77.9	64.6	63.5	78.4	74.1	74.7	75.9	70.0	65.6	74.5	74.4
1969	75.7	76.7	65.5	62.0	77.0	73.0	74.1	75.3	69.3	64.6	74.3	73.5
Aged 15–24												
1966	79.1	80.2	68.0	68.3	82.8	79.4	83.2	82.2	76.2	71.2	77.6	79.0
1967	78.2	79.7	64.1	68.0	80.8	78.9	82.0	80.6	75.1	70.5	76.4	77.9
1968	76.0	77.6	60.9	64.8	78.6	77.1	79.5	78.1	72.0	67.5	74.2	75.5
1969	72.6	73.6	63.2	62.4	73.8	73.7	76.9	76.2	70.7	64.5	72.6	72.4
Aged 25–44												
1966	89.9	91.2	76.1	77.2	93.5	84.7	88.9	87.7	82.8	79.8	87.6	87.6
1967	88.3	89.6	74.3	75.2	91.7	84.4	85.7	86.3	80.3	77.8	87.7	86.2
1968	88.4	89.9	73.1	75.3	88.9	83.1	84.4	86.2	77.5	77.1	88.1	85.4
1969	87.3	88.8	71.9	73.3	88.0	82.4	84.8	85.8	77.3	76.1	86.7	84.6
Aged 45–64												
1966	88.8	89.6	80.2	75.6	88.8	84.6	86.0	86.7	85.4	78.3	84.9	86.0
1967	88.2	88.9	80.5	75.1	86.6	87.6	83.8	86.7	85.8	77.4	84.8	85.4
1968	88.0	88.7	81.3	75.0	86.8	86.2	84.1	86.8	84.6	77.1	84.4	85.2
1969	88.2	88.7	83.0	74.2	87.1	86.0	84.4	87.2	84.0	78.0	85.9	85.5
Aged 65 and over												
1966	21.7	22.5	14.1	14.1	25.1	18.3	19.4	19.5	12.4	11.7	17.6	19.1
1967	20.9	21.5	15.9	14.3	21.5	18.6	18.4	19.3	11.5	10.0	17.6	18.4
1968	19.8	20.4	14.4	12.1	20.6	16.3	17.7	16.8	10.6	9.9	16.0	17.1
1969	20.9	21.4	16.1	11.8	19.4	17.2	17.4	16.8	11.0	10.3	17.4	17.4

Females

Aged 15 and over

Year												
1966	43.1	44.0	33.4	32.5	44.0	39.6	40.0	43.0	34.6	30.2	40.3	40.5
1967	42.6	43.5	33.1	32.1	42.8	40.0	38.8	42.1	34.5	29.5	40.0	40.0
1968	42.5	43.4	33.1	32.2	42.6	39.3	38.8	42.1	34.8	30.1	40.4	39.9
1969	42.6	43.3	35.1	32.5	42.7	39.6	39.3	42.3	35.5	30.1	40.9	40.2
1970	42.5	43.2	35.5	32.5	42.3	40.2	39.3	41.7	36.1	30.5	40.9	40.1

Aged 15–24

Year												
1966	71.2	72.0	61.9	57.4	67.6	66.7	66.4	69.3	66.5	53.6	64.2	67.3
1967	70.0	71.0	58.6	57.3	65.7	67.6	64.5	68.3	63.2	51.3	64.2	66.1
1968	68.3	69.3	57.3	54.2	63.5	63.3	62.2	65.0	63.2	52.6	64.8	64.3
1969	67.2	68.0	59.3	55.5	61.7	62.2	61.2	63.8	62.3	51.3	63.8	63.3
1970	65.5	66.1	58.8	53.8	61.3	63.9	60.9	61.0	61.5	50.8	63.6	62.1

Aged 25–44

Year												
1966	46.9	48.1	34.5	35.6	46.3	41.4	43.7	48.0	36.8	34.0	44.9	44.2
1967	46.4	47.5	33.5	35.0	44.4	41.5	42.9	46.7	37.0	34.8	44.6	43.6
1968	46.8	47.7	37.8	35.0	44.3	41.3	43.4	47.6	37.4	34.6	44.1	43.8
1969	47.9	48.8	38.9	36.3	45.8	42.6	44.1	49.2	39.3	35.6	45.6	45.1
1970	48.6	49.4	40.2	37.5	45.1	43.0	44.8	49.7	40.6	36.4	45.6	45.6

Aged 45–59

Year												
1966	52.3	53.3	40.7	40.7	52.8	47.8	47.4	53.9	36.9	35.3	46.4	48.7
1967	52.2	53.1	41.4	40.6	52.5	48.7	47.0	53.9	38.7	33.5	47.2	48.7
1968	53.3	54.3	41.8	42.6	54.4	50.2	47.9	55.5	39.4	35.4	49.5	50.1
1969	53.5	54.3	44.4	43.0	54.2	50.6	49.0	55.4	41.3	35.8	50.8	50.6
1970	53.9	54.7	45.1	43.1	54.6	52.3	49.8	54.7	43.3	37.1	51.4	51.2

Aged 60 and over

Year												
1966	11.9	12.2	8.0	7.6	12.5	10.0	10.4	10.3	6.9	6.1	10.1	10.4
1967	11.9	12.2	8.4	7.5	11.8	10.2	9.6	9.8	7.4	5.6	9.9	10.2
1968	11.5	12.1	4.9	8.0	11.5	9.8	9.9	9.8	7.6	6.2	10.1	10.1
1969	11.6	11.9	8.0	7.9	11.6	9.6	10.6	10.2	7.5	6.2	10.4	10.3
1970	11.7	12.0	8.4	7.5	11.7	10.1	10.3	10.3	7.1	6.4	10.1	10.3

*The South East of England is a grouping of the South East and East Anglia.

Source: *Department of Employment Gazette.*

explained by any increase which may have taken place in either 'voluntary' or 'false' unemployment (discussed in the next section), since people in these categories will have registered as unemployed and will be included as employees in Table 11.

The Department of Employment has attempted, in an article in the *Gazette* of June 1970, to analyse the reasons for the fall in the working population. There had then been a recorded fall of just over 400,000 between June 1966 and June 1969. Among the reasons put forward the article emphasised the larger proportion of young people in full-time education, changes in the sex- and age-composition of the population, the trend towards earlier marriage and child bearing, and earlier retirement. The article also drew attention to an increase between 1966 and 1968 of 15,000 men between the ages of 45 and 64 classified as 'long-term sick'. (This again underlines the importance of the suggestion put forward in Section 4 that there should be a separate register for people not suitable for normal and regular work.)

No doubt all these factors have continued to have some importance in recent years. But in the light of the further fall of nearly 600,000 in the working population it seems doubtful whether the explanations put forward are adequate to account for all that has taken place more recently. For instance, a smaller *proportion* of men over 65 and women over 60 working does not mean that there are fewer working pensioners, as Table 12 shows.

Table 12

ANNUAL CHANGES IN NUMBER OF EMPLOYEES: 1966 to 1970

(*thousands*)

	Men	of which	Married Women	of which	Other Women	of which
	Total	over 65	Total	over 60	Total	over 6
June 1966–1967	−167	− 6	+ 42	+13	−135	−15
June 1967–1968	−156	−26	+121	+13	−107	−11
June 1968–1969	−138	+17	+158	+18	− 89	+ 2
June 1969–1970	−160	− 4	+133	+15	−129	−13

Source: *British Labour Statistics: Year Book 1969*, Table 93; *Department of Employment Gazette.*

Indeed, more married women over 60 have been remaining at work year by year and the reduction in employment of men over 65 between 1966 and 1970 was only 19,000.

The fall in the working population seems even more remarkable in the light of the substantial number of immigrant workers who have come to Britain since 1966, most of whom were probably between 25 and 44, where the fall in numbers has been particularly baffling. We shall have to wait for the results of the 1971 Census for an official estimate of such workers.

Increase in numbers 'self-employed'?

One explanation for the fall in the working population mentioned in the June 1970 article, but perhaps not given enough weight, is the possibility that there has been a substantial unrecorded increase in the numbers of self-employed. Official statistics of 'employers and self-employed' are particularly unsatisfactory, as they depend on the Census of Population rather than on national insurance records. As the *Gazette* comments 'It is not practicable to estimate short-term changes in the number of self-employed persons', though an attempt to extrapolate figures since the 1966 Census has been made by the Department. Until the results of the 1971 Census are available the extrapolation must remain tentative.

The extrapolation (based on the changes in the number of Class 2 contributors to the National Insurance scheme) is on a very modest scale. The national figures for 'employers and self-employed' since 1966 are:

June	Men	Women
	(thousands)	
1966	1,251	361
1967	1,320	361
1968	1,320	361
1969	1,383	361
1970	1,386	361

Since 1966 the Department has not allowed for any increase in the number of self-employed women, partly because most are likely to have opted out of the National Insurance scheme. The increase of only 130,000 self-employed men is almost certainly much too small. The chief reason for supposing so is that high personal taxation and the growing discontent with the difference between gross pay and take-home pay has gradually persuaded more people to try to become self-employed, and therefore Schedule 'D' rather than Schedule 'E' taxpayers. Employers have no reason to resist. The whole process was clearly summed up by Mr John Silkin (then Minister of Public Building and Works) in the debate on the Construction Industry Contracts Bill on 27 April, 1970:

'Current pressures to adopt self-employed status are mainly of a financial kind. Charges avoided by an employer if his men assume self-employed status include SET, the employer's share

53

of national insurance and National Health Service contributions, redundancy fund contributions, and payment for annual and public holidays. He is also relieved of the necessity of obtaining employers' liability insurance cover, of contributing to redundancy payments if redundancy occurs, of making wages up to a guaranteed weekly minimum under the national working rules, or paying sick pay. The self-employed man's own national insurance contribution is, of course, lower than that of an employee. In addition to these legitimate avoidance factors, there is under the self-employed system an opportunity for the unscrupulous to evade income tax.'[1]

Two industries are particularly concerned—catering and construction. The construction industry certainly presents a very strange picture in the last five years. The number of operatives has fallen by 300,000, unemployment has doubled, while the value of its output has increased substantially in both money and real terms, as Table 13 shows.

Table 13
OUTPUT AND EMPLOYMENT IN THE CONSTRUCTION INDUSTRY, 1965 TO 1971

	Value of output (£ million)	Number employed (thousands)	Output per head (£)
1965	3,302	1,126	2,932
1966	3,450	1,102	3,131
1967	3,654	1,059	3,286
1968	3,881	1,025	3,474
1969	3,993	976	3,860
1970	4,188	881	4,661
1971	4,588	824*	5,568*

*Provisional.
Source: *Monthly Digest of Statistics,* Tables 20 and 105.

In this industry the practice known as 'the Lump' has become notorious. It has been estimated that perhaps 250,000 building workers are 'on the Lump', which means that they work as self-employed builders, sub-contracted to large concerns in ways which have apparently escaped the reach of the tax authorities or national insurance records, though new measures are now in force to stop the abuse.

No estimate is possible of the numbers employed in catering who are not recorded in any figures.

[1] House of Commons *Weekly Hansard,* 28 April, 1970, col. 893.

We have here therefore evidence not of hidden unemployment but of hidden employment. The working population will be under-estimated to the extent that there are people working either without national insurance cards, or as self-employed, whose numbers have yet to be revealed by the 1971 Population Census.

How much hidden unemployment?

Hidden unemployment largely concerns married women. Depending on how they are insured, they may not be entitled to unemployment benefit, and if so, they will have no incentive to register except for the prospect of a new job. No estimate is possible of the numbers who might be willing to work. The official view seems to be that if they do not register, they are not seriously seeking work. In any case, as Table 10 shows, the female working population has fallen very little; it is the decline in the male labour force which is much more striking.

Is there hidden unemployment among men? Are there substantial numbers who have left the labour force, and who have not registered for employment? It may be, for instance, that because the labour exchanges operate in such a restricted segment of the whole labour market, many would-be workers are discouraged from or uninterested in using them.

But why do such men fail to register as unemployed, since there are substantial advantages in doing so? Indeed by not registering they are foregoing not only unemployment and earnings-related benefit, but also such supplementary benefit as may be available. They also lose the opportunity to have their insurance card franked. Unless this enigma can be resolved, the same comment must apply as for women, that anyone seriously seeking work will take the trouble to register for it.

To sum up, the hidden work force consists of those in hidden employment (largely due to under-estimation of the numbers of self-employed) and some hidden unemployment, largely among married women and others for whom registration holds no benefit. While no accurate estimate is possible, the order of magnitude might well be from a quarter up to half-a-million.

SEVEN

The New Unemployed

Some men registered as unemployed are working, and others are unemployed because they are better off not working. No estimates are available or perhaps possible of the extent of such 'false' or 'voluntary' unemployment. All that can be said with certainty is that both exist, and any examination of the labour market must distinguish them from 'involuntary' unemployment.

'Voluntary' unemployment

'Voluntary' unemployment means, for most people, preferring to live on social benefits to having a job. It is only slowly being realised that, depending on family circumstances, the level of earnings, and the time of year, some heads of family may have a financial incentive to stay out of work. A married man with two children under 11 and weekly earnings of £30 will take home as much money for the last 20 weeks of the tax year out of work as in work. A man with four children and only £15 a week would find that for 25 weeks, almost the last half of the tax year, he could marginally increase his income by not working.[1] The cost of employment, for example, travel to and from work, the extra wear and tear on clothing, etc., may make this margin decisive, particularly if there is an opportunity of picking up a few odd jobs paid in (untaxed) cash.

A wide range of cases, from a few weeks to about six months, exists in which income will be higher by not working. As long as PAYE is based on cumulative and not on current receipts, and as long as social benefits are not taxed, this anomalous situation will continue.

Social benefits alone seldom have the effect of making the worker better off out of employment. The refund of tax does, which is why the lowest-paid workers are least likely to be those taking advantage of the system, as they will not be entitled to much or any tax refund.

It is not possible to put a figure on the number of voluntarily unemployed. They certainly form some part of recorded unemploy-

---

[1] These examples were chosen before the 1972 Budget.

ment. Deliberate exploitation is probably limited, however, because even those who try will have to be certain they can find fresh employment immediately after the end of the tax year in April. If they fail, they will not accumulate earnings, and therefore tax, to be refunded in the following year.

Difficulties will remain because benefits are national but wage levels (and prices) vary from region to region. As the manager of one employment exchange in a low-wage area was reported in the Press early in 1972 as saying:

> 'My staff are constantly facing the moral dilemma of trying to place people in work when the likely wages can be lower than the amount of unemployment benefit and social security payments a man could draw. They are asking men, in fact, to accept a cut in real income.'[1]

The rising cost of unemployment support

These circumstances naturally tend to reduce the numbers in recorded active employment, and at a considerable cost to society. Chart 3 shows how this cost has grown since 1949. The unbroken black line shows the total spending on unemployment benefit and earnings-related supplements, excluding the cost of administration, together with supplementary benefits to unemployed persons, and redundancy payments since they were introduced at the end of 1965. The broken line on the Chart shows the wholly unemployed during the same period. It is, of course, right that help should be given to people involuntarily unemployed, and given so that unemployment is no longer identified with poverty. But clearly the relationship between the level of unemployment and the amount spent to relieve it has changed markedly, even allowing for the fall in the value of money. The cost has increased both because there are more people out of work, and because rates of assistance have been improved.[2] The contrast would be even more striking if all who were wholly unemployed claimed benefit, whereas about a quarter do not, either because they choose not to or because they are ineligible.

In 1971 the amount spent on supporting the unemployed was about £500 million, about equal to the whole amount for the years 1949 to 1961. It is inevitable that provision on this scale makes an impact on the labour market. More ample social benefits must—and indeed were to some extent intended to—enable people who lose

---

[1]*Daily Telegraph*, 3 February, 1972.

[2]Unemployment benefit was raised in January 1965, October 1967, November 1969 and September 1971. Earnings-related benefit was not available until October 1966. The first payments under the Redundancy Payments Act were made in December 1965.

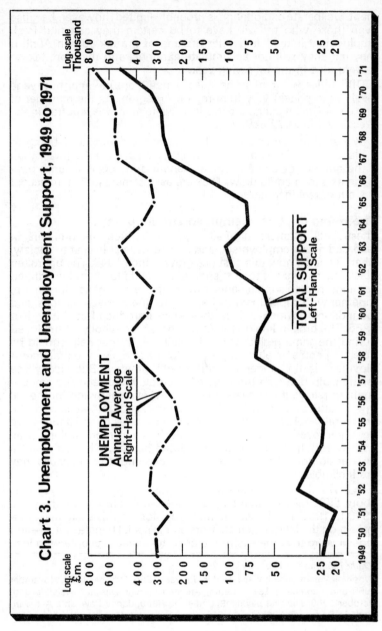

Chart 3. Unemployment and Unemployment Support, 1949 to 1971

their jobs at least to take more time to find new employment. Some increase in the duration of unemployment was bound to follow. Moreover, the increase in unemployment has the further consequence that some people are now discovering for the first time, and by accident, that they are better off on social benefit than in employment.

Where the balance of 'political' or 'social' advantage lies is not the concern of this *Monograph*. What matters for the purpose of studying the measurement of unemployment is that the supply price of labour must have been changed by the increase in financial help to the unemployed since 1966.

High benefit rates encourage fraud

More ample provision of benefits, particularly supplementary benefits, not perhaps matched by more surveillance, has had the further consequence that they are now proving an incentive to make false claims to be unemployed.

Again, the construction and catering industries are particularly affected. In catering temporary work is easily available and day-to-day engagement is not unusual. This practice can be continued without an insurance card, which can therefore be deposited at the labour exchange if the worker is trying simultaneously to draw benefit.

Similarly in construction, where nearly 150,000 were reported unemployed at the end of 1971, men are said to be registered as unemployed, drawing benefit, and at the same time working part-time or even full-time for cash.[1]

Of course, this practice is illegal, but it can be stopped only by stricter control. Where special checks have been made in particular towns, such as Brixton and Southend, the numbers registered as unemployed have fallen dramatically. Though no estimate can be given of the full extent of abuse, a revealing insight may be found in the 1970 Annual Report of the Department of Health and Social Security (para. 11.44). The number of specialist 'unemploy-

---

[1] In the House of Commons debate on the Construction Industry Contracts Bill (27 April, 1970), Mr E. S. Heffer related how a bricklayer constituent of his went to a site near Liverpool where about 150 operatives were employed. 'He found that on Thursday and Friday afternoons he was practically on his own. The site was a sort of desert. Everyone disappeared. When he asked where they had all gone, he was told that they had gone to draw their dole'. Later Mr Heffer added '. . . the unemployment figures are inflated because, with the labour-only system, some people have been drawing unemployment benefit whilst at the same time carrying on with labour-only work'. (House of Commons *Weekly Hansard*, 27 April, 1970, col. 928.)

ment review officers' attached to regional offices was doubled from 60 to 120 in 1970, and a scrutiny of unemployment claims in the single month from 18 November to 15 December, 1970, had the following results:

'Some 7,375 claimants ceased to draw a supplementary allowance after being called for a special interview. About 2,400 of them did so before the interview was due to take place; 3,750 found or were placed in employment after interview and 1,225 had their allowances limited or withdrawn because it was considered that suitable work was available for them'.

A further increase in the amount of scrutiny and investigation by the inspectorates of the Department of Employment and the Department of Health and Social Security will no doubt be necessary to reduce the numbers in 'false' unemployment to insignificant levels.

How much 'involuntary' unemployment?

Only at this late stage is it becoming possible to examine with any confidence real 'involuntary' unemployment.

As explained in Section 2, allowance has to be made for the redeployment of labour, and, in Section 4, for the number of unemployables. After this is done these further categories of 'false' and 'voluntary' unemployment must also be taken into account even though no quantification has yet been attempted. The figure which remained would still include the prematurely retired who register merely to have their National Insurance card franked. The number in this group is again not known, but unlikely to be less than 30,000.

What remains at the end of all these adjustments could be described as 'involuntary' unemployment due to structural and cyclical changes in the economy.[1] But even here it should be noted that this description implicitly assumes that labour is and should be treated as immobile. Some at least of the 'involuntarily' unemployed could find new jobs if they were prepared to change their homes or occupations.

---

[1] On the distinction between descriptions of unemployment on empirical and on logical criteria, Professor W. H. Hutt, *The Theory of Idle Resources*, Jonathan Cape, 1939.